Mercenary

by

Mack Reynolds

MERCENARY
by MACK REYNOLDS

Copyright © 2023

ISBN: 978-93-59325-59-0

Published by

DOUBLE 9 BOOKS

2/13-B, Ansari Road, Daryaganj
New Delhi – 110002
info@double9books.com
www.double9books.com
Tel. 011-40042856

ABOUT THE AUTHOR

Dallas McCord "Mack" Reynolds (November 11, 1917 – January 30, 1983) was a science fiction writer from the United States. Dallas Ross, Mark Mallory, Clark Collins, Dallas Rose, Guy McCord, Maxine Reynolds, Bob Belmont, and Todd Harding were some of his pen names. His work was primarily concerned with socioeconomic speculation, which he communicated through thought-provoking studies of utopian society from a radical, often satiric standpoint. From the 1950s until the 1970s, he was a popular author, particularly among readers of science fiction and fantasy periodicals. Reynolds was the first author to create an original novel based on the NBC television series Star Trek, which aired from 1966 to 1969. Mission to Horatius (1968) was written for young readers. Reynolds was the second of four children born to Verne La Rue Reynolds and Pauline McCord in Corcoran, California. Reynolds was schooled to support the concepts of Marxism and socialism by his father, who joined the Socialist Labor Party (SLP) after the family relocated to Baltimore in 1918. ("I grew up in a Marxist-Socialist family. "I am the child who, when he was five or six years old, asked his mother, 'Mother, who is Comrade Jesus Christ?' —because I had never met anyone in that household who wasn't called Comrade." Reynolds joined the SLP in 1935, while still in high school in Kingston, New York, and quickly became an ardent supporter of the party's ideals.

CONTENTS

Joseph Mauser spotted the recruiting line-up from two or three blocks down the street, shortly after driving into Kingston. The local offices of Vacuum Tube Transport, undoubtedly. Baron Haer would be doing his recruiting for the fracas with Continental Hovercraft there if for no other reason than to save on rents. The Baron was watching pennies on this one and that was bad.

In fact, it was so bad that even as Joe Mauser let his sports hovercar sink to a parking level and vaulted over its side he was still questioning his decision to sign up with the Vacuum Tube outfit rather than with their opponents. Joe was an old pro and old pros do not get to be old pros in the Category Military without developing an instinct to stay away from losing sides.

Fine enough for Low-Lowers and Mid-Lowers to sign up with this outfit, as opposed to that, motivated by no other reasoning than the snappiness of the uniform and the stock shares offered, but an old pro considered carefully such matters as budget. Baron Haer was watching every expense, was, it was rumored, figuring on commanding himself and calling upon relatives and friends for his staff. Continental Hovercraft, on the other hand, was heavy with variable capital and was in a position to hire Stonewall Cogswell himself for their tactician.

However, the die was cast. You didn't run up a caste level, not to speak of two at once, by playing it careful. Joe had planned this out; for once, old pro or not, he was taking risks.

Recruiting line-ups were not for such as he. Not for many a year, many a fracas. He strode rapidly along this one, heading for the offices ahead, noting only in passing the quality of the men who were taking service with Vacuum Tube Transport. These were the soldiers he'd be commanding in the immediate future and the prospects looked grim. There were few veterans among them. Their stance, their demeanor, their ... well, you could tell a veteran even though he be Rank Private. You could tell a veteran of even one fracas. It showed.

He knew the situation. The word had gone out. Baron Malcolm Haer was due for a defeat. You weren't going to pick up any lush bonuses signing up with him, and you definitely weren't going to jump a caste. In short, no matter what Haer's past record, choose what was going to be the winning side—Continental Hovercraft. Continental Hovercraft and old Stonewall

Cogswell who had lost so few fracases that many a Telly buff couldn't remember a single one.

Individuals among these men showed promise, Joe Mauser estimated even as he walked, but promise means little if you don't live long enough to cash in on it.

Take that small man up ahead. He'd obviously got himself into a hassle maintaining his place in line against two or three heftier would-be soldiers. The little fellow wasn't backing down a step in spite of the attempts of the other Lowers to usurp his place. Joe Mauser liked to see such spirit. You could use it when you were in the dill.

As he drew abreast of the altercation, he snapped from the side of his mouth, "Easy, lads. You'll get all the scrapping you want with Hovercraft. Wait until then."

He'd expected his tone of authority to be enough, even though he was in mufti. He wasn't particularly interested in the situation, beyond giving the little man a hand. A veteran would have recognized him as an old-timer and probable officer, and heeded, automatically.

These evidently weren't veterans.

"Says who?" one of the Lowers growled back at him. "You one of Baron Haer's kids, or something?"

Joe Mauser came to a halt and faced the other. He was irritated, largely with himself. He didn't want to be bothered. Nevertheless, there was no alternative now.

The line of men, all Lowers so far as Joe could see, had fallen silent in an expectant hush. They were bored with their long wait. Now something would break the monotony.

By tomorrow, Joe Mauser would be in command of some of these men. In as little as a week he would go into a full-fledged fracas with them. He couldn't afford to lose face. Not even at this point when all, including himself, were still civilian garbed. When matters pickled, in a fracas, you wanted men with complete confidence in you.

The man who had grumbled the surly response was a near physical twin of Joe Mauser which put him in his early thirties, gave him five foot eleven of altitude and about one hundred and eighty pounds. His clothes casted him Low-Lower—nothing to lose. As with many who have nothing to lose, he was willing to risk all for principle. His face now registered that ideal. Joe Mauser had no authority over him, nor his friends.

Joe's eyes flicked to the other two who had been pestering the little fellow. They weren't quite so aggressive and as yet had come to no conclusion about their stand. Probably the three had been unacquainted before their bullying alliance to deprive the smaller man of his place. However, a moment of hesitation and Joe would have a trio on his hands.

He went through no further verbal preliminaries. Joe Mauser stepped closer. His right hand lanced forward, not doubled in a fist but fingers close together and pointed, spear-like. He sank it into the other's abdomen, immediately below the rib cage—the solar plexus.

He had misestimated the other two. Even as his opponent crumpled, they were upon him, coming in from each side. And at least one of them, he could see now, had been in hand-to-hand combat before. In short, another pro, like Joe himself.

He took one blow, rolling with it, and his feet automatically went into the shuffle of the trained fighter. He retreated slightly to erect defenses, plan attack. They pressed him strongly, sensing victory in his retreat.

The one mattered little to him. Joe Mauser could have polished off the oaf in a matter of seconds, had he been allotted seconds to devote. But the second, the experienced one, was the problem. He and Joe were well matched and with the oaf as an ally really he had all the best of it.

Support came from a forgotten source, the little chap who had been the reason for the whole hassle. He waded in now as big as the next man so far as spirit was concerned, but a sorry fate gave him to attack the wrong man, the veteran rather than the tyro. He took a crashing blow to the side of his head which sent him sailing back into the recruiting line, now composed of excited, shouting verbal participants of the fray.

However, the extinction of Joe Mauser's small ally had taken a moment or two and time was what Joe needed most. For a double second he had the oaf alone on his hands and that was sufficient. He caught a flailing arm, turned his back and automatically went into the movements which result in that spectacular hold of the wrestler, the Flying Mare. Just in time he recalled that his opponent was a future comrade-in-arms and twisted the arm so that it bent at the elbow, rather than breaking. He hurled the other over his shoulder and as far as possible, to take the scrap out of him, and twirled quickly to meet the further attack of his sole remaining foe.

That phase of the combat failed to materialize.

A voice of command bit out, "Hold it, you lads!"

The original situation which had precipitated the fight was being duplicated. But while the three Lowers had failed to respond to Joe Mauser's tone of authority, there was no similar failure now.

The owner of the voice, beautifully done up in the uniform of Vacuum Tube Transport, complete to kilts and the swagger stick of the officer of Rank Colonel or above, stood glaring at them. Age, Joe estimated, even as he came to attention, somewhere in the late twenties — an Upper in caste. Born to command. His face holding that arrogant, contemptuous expression once common to the patricians of Rome, the Prussian Junkers, the British ruling class of the Nineteenth Century. Joe knew the expression well. How well he knew it. On more than one occasion, he had dreamt of it.

Joe said, "Yes, sir."

"What in Zen goes on here? Are you lads overtranked?"

"No, sir," Joe's veteran opponent grumbled, his eyes on the ground, a schoolboy before the principal.

Joe said, evenly, "A private disagreement, sir."

"Disagreement!" the Upper snorted. His eyes went to the three fallen combatants, who were in various stages of reviving. "I'd hate to see you lads in a real scrap."

That brought a response from the non-combatants in the recruiting line. The *bon mot* wasn't that good but caste has its privileges and the laughter was just short of uproarious.

Which seemed to placate the kilted officer. He tapped his swagger stick against the side of his leg while he ran his eyes up and down Joe Mauser and the others, as though memorizing them for future reference.

"All right," he said. "Get back into the line, and you trouble makers quiet down. We're processing as quickly as we can." And at that point he added insult to injury with an almost word for word repetition of what Joe had said a few moments earlier. "You'll get all the fighting you want from Hovercraft, if you can wait until then."

The four original participants of the rumpus resumed their places in various stages of sheepishness. The little fellow, nursing an obviously aching jaw, made a point of taking up his original position even while darting a look of thanks to Joe Mauser who still stood where he had when the fight was interrupted.

The Upper looked at Joe. "Well, lad, are you interested in signing up with Vacuum Tube Transport or not?"

"Yes, sir," Joe said evenly. Then, "Joseph Mauser, sir. Category Military, Rank Captain."

"Indeed." The officer looked him up and down all over again, his nostrils high. "A Middle, I assume. And brawling with recruits." He held a long silence. "Very well, come with me." He turned and marched off.

Joe inwardly shrugged. This was a fine start for his pitch — a fine start. He had half a mind to give it all up, here and now, and head on up to Catskill to enlist with Continental Hovercraft. His big scheme would wait for another day. Nevertheless, he fell in behind the aristocrat and followed him to the offices which had been his original destination.

Two Rank Privates with 45-70 Springfields and wearing the Haer kilts in such wise as to indicate permanent status in Vacuum Tube Transport came to the salute as they approached. The Upper preceding Joe Mauser flicked his swagger stick in an easy nonchalance. Joe felt envious amusement. How long did it take to learn how to answer a salute with that degree of arrogant ease?

There were desks in here, and typers humming, as Vacuum Tube Transport office workers, mobilized for this special service, processed volunteers for the company forces. Harried noncoms and junior-grade officers buzzed everywhere, failing miserably to bring order to the chaos. To the right was a door with a medical cross newly painted on it. When it occasionally popped open to admit or emit a recruit, white-robed doctors, male nurses and half nude men could be glimpsed beyond.

Joe followed the other through the press and to an inner office at which door he didn't bother to knock. He pushed his way through, waved in greeting with his swagger stick to the single occupant who looked up from the paper- and tape-strewn desk at which he sat.

Joe Mauser had seen the face before on Telly though never so tired as this and never with the element of defeat to be read in the expression. Bullet-headed, barrel-figured Baron Malcolm Haer of Vacuum Tube Transport. Category Transportation, Mid-Upper, and strong candidate for Upper-Upper upon retirement. However, there would be few who expected retirement in the immediate future. Hardly. Malcolm Haer found too obvious a lusty enjoyment in the competition between Vacuum Tube Transport and its stronger rivals.

Joe came to attention, bore the sharp scrutiny of his chosen commander-to-be. The older man's eyes went to the kilted Upper officer who had brought Joe along. "What is it, Balt?"

The other gestured with his stick at Joe. "Claims to be Rank Captain. Looking for a commission with us, Dad. I wouldn't know why." The last sentence was added lazily.

The older Haer shot an irritated glance at his son. "Possibly for the same reason mercenaries usually enlist for a fracas, Balt." His eyes came back to Joe.

Joe Mauser, still at attention even though in mufti, opened his mouth to give his name, category and rank, but the older man waved a hand negatively. "Captain Mauser, isn't it? I caught the fracas between Carbonaceous Fuel and United Miners, down on the Panhandle Reservation. Seems to me I've spotted you once or twice before, too."

"Yes, sir," Joe said. This was some improvement in the way things were going.

The older Haer was scowling at him. "Confound it, what are you doing with no more rank than captain? On the face of it, you're an old hand, a highly experienced veteran."

An old pro, we call ourselves, Joe said to himself. *Old pros, we call ourselves, among ourselves.*

Aloud, he said, "I was born a Mid-Lower, sir."

There was understanding in the old man's face, but Balt Haer said loftily, "What's that got to do with it? Promotion is quick and based on merit in Category Military."

At a certain point, if you are good combat officer material, you speak your mind no matter the rank of the man you are addressing. On this occasion, Joe Mauser needed few words. He let his eyes go up and down Balt Haer's immaculate uniform, taking in the swagger stick of the Rank Colonel or above. Joe said evenly, "Yes, sir."

Balt Haer flushed quick temper. "What do you mean by —"

But his father was chuckling. "You have spirit, captain. I need spirit now. You are quite correct. My son, though a capable officer, I assure you, has probably not participated in a fraction of the fracases you have to your credit. However, there is something to be said for the training available to we Uppers in the academies. For instance, captain, have you ever commanded a body of lads larger than, well, a *company*?"

Joe said flatly, "In the Douglas-Boeing versus Lockheed-Cessna fracas we took a high loss of officers when the Douglas-Boeing outfit rang in some fast-firing French *mitrailleuse* we didn't know they had. As my superiors took casualties I was field promoted to acting battalion commander, to acting regimental commander, to acting brigadier. For three days I held the rank of acting commander of brigade. We won."

Balt Haer snapped his fingers. "I remember that. Read quite a paper on it." He eyed Joe Mauser, almost respectfully. "Stonewall Cogswell got the credit for the victory and received his marshal's baton as a result."

"He was one of the few other officers that survived," Joe said dryly.

"But, Zen! You mean you got no promotion at all?"

Joe said, "I was upped to Low-Middle from High-Lower, sir. At my age, at the time, quite a promotion."

Baron Haer was remembering, too. "That was the fracas that brought on the howl from the Sovs. They claimed those *mitrailleuse* were post-1900 and violated the Universal Disarmament Pact. Yes, I recall that. Douglas-Boeing was able to prove that the weapon was used by the French as far back as the Franco-Prussian War." He eyed Joe with new interest now. "Sit down, captain. You too, Balt. Do you realize that Captain Mauser is the only recruit of officer rank we've had today?"

"Yes," the younger Haer said dryly. "However, it's too late to call the fracas off now. Hovercraft wouldn't stand for it, and the Category Military Department would back them. Our only alternative is unconditional surrender, and you know what that means."

"It means our family would probably be forced from control of the firm," the older man growled. "But nobody has suggested surrender on any terms. Nobody, thus far." He glared at his officer son who took it with an easy shrug and swung a leg over the edge of his father's desk in the way of a seat.

Joe Mauser found a chair and lowered himself into it. Evidently, the foppish Balt Haer had no illusions about the spot his father had got the family corporation into. And the younger man was right, of course.

But the Baron wasn't blind to reality any more than he was a coward. He dismissed Balt Haer's defeatism from his mind and came back to Joe Mauser. "As I say, you're the only officer recruit today. Why?"

Joe said evenly, "I wouldn't know, sir. Perhaps freelance Category Military men are occupied elsewhere. There's always a shortage of trained officers."

Baron Haer was waggling a finger negatively. "That's not what I mean, captain. You are an old hand. This is your category and you must know it well. Then why are *you* signing up with Vacuum Tube Transport rather than Hovercraft?"

Joe Mauser looked at him for a moment without speaking.

"Come, come, captain. I am an old hand too, in my category, and not a fool. I realize there is scarcely a soul in the West-world that expects anything but disaster for my colors. Pay rates have been widely posted. I can offer only five common shares of Vacuum Tube for a Rank Captain, win or lose. Hovercraft is doubling that, and can pick and choose among the best officers in the hemisphere."

Joe said softly, "I have all the shares I need."

Balt Haer had been looking back and forth between his father and the newcomer and becoming obviously more puzzled. He put in, "Well, what in Zen motivates you if it isn't the stock we offer?"

Joe glanced at the younger Haer to acknowledge the question but he spoke to the Baron. "Sir, like you said, you're no fool. However, you've been sucked in, this time. When you took on Hovercraft, you were thinking in terms of a regional dispute. You wanted to run one of your vacuum tube deals up to Fairbanks from Edmonton. You were expecting a minor fracas, involving possibly five thousand men. You never expected Hovercraft to parlay it up, through their connections in the Category Military Department, to a divisional magnitude fracas which you simply aren't large enough to afford. But Hovercraft was getting sick of your corporation. You've been nicking away at them too long. So they decided to do you in. They've hired Marshal Cogswell and the best combat officers in North America, and they're hiring the most competent veterans they can find. Every fracas buff who watches Telly, figures you've had it. They've been watching you come up the aggressive way, the hard way, for a long time, but now they're all going to be sitting on the edges of their sofas waiting for you to get it."

Baron Haer's heavy face had hardened as Joe Mauser went on relentlessly. He growled, "Is this what everyone thinks?"

"Yes. Everyone intelligent enough to have an opinion." Joe made a motion of his head to the outer offices where the recruiting was proceeding. "Those men out there are rejects from Catskill, where old Baron Zwerdling is recruiting. Either that or they're inexperienced Low-Lowers, too stupid to realize they're sticking their necks out. Not one man in ten is a veteran. And when things begin to pickle, you want veterans."

Baron Malcolm Haer sat back in his chair and stared coldly at Captain Joe Mauser. He said, "At first I was moderately surprised that an old time mercenary like yourself should choose my uniform, rather than Zwerdling's. Now I am increasingly mystified about motivation. So all over again I ask you, captain: Why are you requesting a commission in my forces which you seem convinced will meet disaster?"

Joe wet his lips carefully. "I think I know a way you can win."

CHAPTER II

His permanent military rank the Haers had no way to alter, but they were short enough of competent officers that they gave him an acting rating and pay scale of major and command of a squadron of cavalry. Joe Mauser wasn't interested in a cavalry command this fracas, but he said nothing. Immediately, he had to size up the situation; it wasn't time as yet to reveal the big scheme. And, meanwhile, they could use him to whip the Rank Privates into shape.

He had left the offices of Baron Haer to go through the red tape involved in being signed up on a temporary basis in the Vacuum Tube Transport forces, and reentered the confusion of the outer offices where the Lowers were being processed and given medicals. He reentered in time to run into a Telly team which was doing a live broadcast.

Joe Mauser remembered the news reporter who headed the team. He'd run into him two or three times in fracases. As a matter of fact, although Joe held the standard Military Category prejudices against Telly, he had a basic respect for this particular newsman. On the occasions he'd seen him before, the fellow was hot in the midst of the action even when things were in the dill. He took as many chances as did the average combatant, and you can't ask for more than that.

The other knew him, too, of course. It was part of his job to be able to spot the celebrities and near celebrities. He zeroed in on Joe now, making flicks of his hand to direct the cameras. Joe, of course, was fully aware of the value of Telly and was glad to co-operate.

"Captain! Captain Mauser, isn't it? Joe Mauser who held out for four days in the swamps of Louisiana with a single company while his ranking officers reformed behind him."

That was one way of putting it, but both Joe and the newscaster who had covered the debacle knew the reality of the situation. When the front had collapsed, his commanders — of Upper caste, of course — had hauled out, leaving him to fight a delaying action while they mended their fences with the enemy, coming to the best terms possible. Yes, that had been the

United Oil versus Allied Petroleum fracas, and Joe had emerged with little either in glory or pelf.

The average fracas fan wasn't on an intellectual level to appreciate anything other than victory. The good guys win, the bad guys lose—that's obvious, isn't it? Not one out of ten Telly followers of the fracases was interested in a well-conducted retreat or holding action. They wanted blood, lots of it, and they identified with the winning side.

Joe Mauser wasn't particularly bitter about this aspect. It was part of his way of life. In fact, his pet peeve was the *real* buff. The type, man or woman, who could remember every fracas you'd ever been in, every time you'd copped one, and how long you'd been in the hospital. Fans who could remember, even better than you could, every time the situation had pickled on you and you'd had to fight your way out as best you could. They'd tell you about it, their eyes gleaming, sometimes a slightest trickle of spittle at the sides of their mouths. They usually wanted an autograph, or a souvenir such as a uniform button.

Now Joe said to the Telly reporter, "That's right, Captain Mauser. Acting major, in this fracas, ah—"

"Freddy. Freddy Soligen. You remember me, captain—"

"Of course I do, Freddy. We've been in the dill, side by side, more than once, and even when I was too scared to use my side arm, you'd be scanning away with your camera."

"Ha ha, listen to the captain, folks. I hope my boss is tuned in. But seriously, Captain Mauser, what do you think the chances of Vacuum Tube Transport are in this fracas?"

Joe looked into the camera lens, earnestly. "The best, of course, or I wouldn't have signed up with Baron Haer, Freddy. Justice triumphs, and anybody who is familiar with the issues in this fracas, knows that Baron Haer is on the side of true right."

Freddy said, holding any sarcasm he must have felt, "What would you say the issues were, captain?"

"The basic North American free enterprise right to compete. Hovercraft has held a near monopoly in transport to Fairbanks. Vacuum Tube Transport wishes to lower costs and bring the consumers of Fairbanks better service through running a vacuum tube to that area. What could be more in the traditions of the West-world? Continental Hovercraft stands in the way and it is they who have demanded of the Category Military Department a trial by arms. On the face of it, justice is on the side of Baron Haer."

Freddy Soligen said into the camera, "Well, all you good people of the Telly world, that's an able summation the captain has made, but it certainly doesn't jibe with the words of Baron Zwerdling we heard this morning, does it? However, justice triumphs and we'll see what the field of combat will have to offer. Thank you, thank you very much, Captain Mauser. All of us, all of us tuned in today, hope that you personally will run into no dill in this fracas."

"Thanks, Freddy. Thanks all," Joe said into the camera, before turning away. He wasn't particularly keen about this part of the job, but you couldn't underrate the importance of pleasing the buffs. In the long run it was your career, your chances for promotion both in military rank and ultimately in caste. It was the way the fans took you up, boosted you, idolized you, worshipped you if you really made it. He, Joe Mauser, was only a minor celebrity, he appreciated every chance he had to be interviewed by such a popular reporter as Freddy Soligen.

Even as he turned, he spotted the four men with whom he'd had his spat earlier. The little fellow was still to the fore. Evidently, the others had decided the one place extra that he represented wasn't worth the trouble he'd put in their way defending it.

On an impulse he stepped up to the small man who began a grin of recognition, a grin that transformed his feisty face. A revelation of an inner warmth beyond average in a world which had lost much of its human warmth.

Joe said, "Like a job, soldier?"

"Name's Max. Max Mainz. Sure I want a job. That's why I'm in this everlasting line."

Joe said, "First fracas for you, isn't it?"

"Yeah, but I had basic training in school."

"What do you weigh, Max?"

Max's face soured. "About one twenty."

"Did you check out on semaphore in school?"

"Well, sure. I'm Category Food, Sub-division Cooking, Branch Chef, but, like I say, I took basic military training, like most everybody else."

"I'm Captain Joe Mauser. How'd you like to be my batman?"

Max screwed up his already not overly handsome face. "Gee, I don't know. I kinda joined up to see some action. Get into the dill. You know what I mean."

Joe said dryly, "See here, Mainz, you'll probably find more pickled situations next to me than you'll want—and you'll come out alive."

The recruiting sergeant looked up from the desk. It was Max Mainz's turn to be processed. The sergeant said, "Lad, take a good opportunity when it drops in your lap. The captain is one of the best in the field. You'll learn more, get better chances for promotion, if you stick with him."

Joe couldn't remember ever having run into the sergeant before, but he said, "Thanks, sergeant."

The other said, evidently realizing Joe didn't recognize him, "We were together on the Chihuahua Reservation, on the jurisdictional fracas between the United Miners and the Teamsters, sir."

It had been almost fifteen years ago. About all that Joe Mauser remembered of that fracas was the abnormal number of casualties they'd taken. His side had lost, but from this distance in time Joe couldn't even remember what force he'd been with. But now he said, "That's right. I thought I recognized you, sergeant."

"It was my first fracas, sir." The sergeant went businesslike. "If you want I should hustle this lad though, captain—"

"Please do, sergeant." Joe added to Max, "I'm not sure where my billet will be. When you're through all this, locate the officer's mess and wait there for me."

"Well, O.K.," Max said doubtfully, still scowling but evidently a servant of an officer, if he wanted to be or not.

"Sir," the sergeant added ominously. "If you've had basic, you know enough how to address an officer."

"Well, yessir," Max said hurriedly.

Joe began to turn away, but then spotted the man immediately behind Max Mainz. He was one of the three with whom Joe had tangled earlier, the one who'd obviously had previous combat experience. He pointed the man out to the sergeant. "You'd better give this lad at least temporary rank of corporal. He's a veteran and we're short of veterans."

The sergeant said, "Yes, sir. We sure are." Joe's former foe looked properly thankful.

Joe Mauser finished off his own red tape and headed for the street to locate a military tailor who could do him up a set of the Haer kilts and fill his other dress requirements. As he went, he wondered vaguely just how many different uniforms he had worn in his time.

In a career as long as his own from time to time you took semi-permanent positions in bodyguards, company police, or possibly the permanent combat troops of this corporation or that. But largely, if you were ambitious, you signed up for the fracases and that meant into a uniform and out of it again in as short a period as a couple of weeks.

At the door he tried to move aside but was too slow for the quick moving young woman who caromed off him. He caught her arm to prevent her from stumbling. She looked at him with less than thanks.

Joe took the blame for the collision. "Sorry," he said. "I'm afraid I didn't see you, Miss."

"Obviously," she said coldly. Her eyes went up and down him, and for a moment he wondered where he had seen her before. Somewhere, he was sure.

She was dressed as they dress who have never considered cost and she had an elusive beauty which would have been even the more hadn't her face projected quite such a serious outlook. Her features were more delicate than those to which he was usually attracted. Her lips were less full, but still— He was reminded of the classic ideal of the British Romantic Period, the women sung of by Byron and Keats, Shelly and Moore.

She said, "Is there any particular reason why you should be staring at me, Mr.—"

"Captain Mauser," Joe said hurriedly. "I'm afraid I've been rude, Miss—Well, I thought I recognized you."

She took in his civilian dress, typed it automatically, and came to an erroneous conclusion. She said, "Captain? You mean that with everyone else I know drawing down ranks from Lieutenant Colonel to Brigadier General, you can't make anything better than Captain?"

Joe winced. He said carefully, "I came up from the ranks, Miss. Captain is quite an achievement, believe me."

"Up from the ranks!" She took in his clothes again. "You mean you're a Middle? You neither talk nor look like a Middle, captain." She used the caste rating as though it was not *quite* a derogatory term.

Not that she meant to be deliberately insulting, Joe knew, wearily. How well he knew. It was simply born in her. As once a well-educated aristocracy had, not necessarily unkindly, named their status inferiors *niggers*; or other aristocrats, in another area of the country, had named theirs *greasers*. Yes, how well he knew.

He said very evenly, "Mid-Middle now, Miss. However, I was born in the Lower castes."

An eyebrow went up. "Zen! You must have put in many an hour studying. You talk like an Upper, captain." She dropped all interest in him and turned to resume her journey.

"Just a moment," Joe said. "You can't go in there, Miss —"

Her eyebrows went up again. "The name is Haer," she said. "Why can't I go in here, captain?"

Now it came to him why he had thought he recognized her. She had basic features similar to those of that overbred poppycock, Balt Haer.

"Sorry," Joe said. "I suppose under the circumstances, you can. I was about to tell you that they're recruiting with lads running around half clothed. Medical inspections, that sort of thing."

She made a noise through her nose and said over her shoulder, even as she sailed on. "Besides being a Haer, I'm an M.D., captain. At the ludicrous sight of a man shuffling about in his shorts, I seldom blush."

She was gone.

Joe Mauser looked after her. "I'll bet you don't," he muttered.

Had she waited a few minutes he could have explained his Upper accent and his unlikely education. When you'd copped one you had plenty of opportunity in hospital beds to read, to study, to contemplate — and to fester away in your own schemes of rebellion against fate. And Joe had copped many in his time.

CHAPTER III

By the time Joe Mauser called it a day and retired to his quarters he was exhausted to the point where his basic dissatisfaction with the trade he followed was heavily upon him.

He had met his immediate senior officers, largely dilettante Uppers with precious little field experience, and was unimpressed. And he'd met his own junior officers and was shocked. By the looks of things at this stage, Captain Mauser's squadron would be going into this fracas both undermanned with Rank Privates and with junior officers composed largely of temporarily promoted noncoms. If this was typical of Baron Haer's total force, then Balt Haer had been correct; unconditional surrender was to be considered, no matter how disastrous to Haer family fortunes.

Joe had been able to take immediate delivery of one kilted uniform. Now, inside his quarters, he began stripping out of his jacket. Somewhat to his surprise, the small man he had selected earlier in the day to be his batman entered from an inner room, also resplendent in the Haer uniform and obviously happily so.

He helped his superior out of the jacket with an ease that held no subservience but at the same time was correctly respectful. You'd have thought him a batman specially trained.

Joe grunted, "Max, isn't it? I'd forgotten about you. Glad you found our billet all right."

Max said, "Yes, sir. Would the captain like a drink? I picked up a bottle of applejack. Applejack's the drink around here, sir. Makes a topnotch highball with ginger ale and a twist of lemon."

Joe Mauser looked at him. Evidently his tapping this man for orderly had been sheer fortune. Well, Joe Mauser could use some good luck on this job. He hoped it didn't end with selecting a batman.

Joe said, "An applejack highball sounds wonderful, Max. Got ice?"

"Of course, sir." Max left the small room.

Joe Mauser and his officers were billeted in what had once been a motel on the old road between Kingston and Woodstock. There was a shower and a tiny kitchenette in each cottage. That was one advantage in a fracas held in an area where there were plenty of facilities. Such military reservations as that of the Little Big Horn in Montana and particularly some of those in the South West and Mexico, were another thing.

Joe lowered himself into the room's easy-chair and bent down to untie his laces. He kicked his shoes off. He could use that drink. He began wondering all over again if his scheme for winning this Vacuum Tube Transport versus Continental Hovercraft fracas would come off. The more he saw of Baron Haer's inadequate forces, the more he wondered. He hadn't expected Vacuum Tube to be in *this* bad a shape. Baron Haer had been riding high for so long that one would have thought his reputation for victory would have lured many a veteran to his colors. Evidently they hadn't bitten. The word was out all right.

Max Mainz returned with the drink.

Joe said, "You had one yourself?"

"No, sir."

Joe said, "Well, Zen, go get yourself one and come on back and sit down. Let's get acquainted."

"Well, yessir." Max disappeared back into the kitchenette to return almost immediately. The little man slid into a chair, drink awkwardly in hand.

His superior sized him up, all over again. Not much more than a kid, really. Surprisingly aggressive for a Lower who must have been raised from childhood in a trank-bemused, Telly-entertained household. The fact that he'd broken away from that environment at all was to his credit, it was considerably easier to conform. But then it is always easier to conform, to run with the herd, as Joe well knew. His own break hadn't been an easy one. "Relax," he said now.

Max said, "Well, this is my first day."

"I know. And you've been seeing Telly shows all your life showing how an orderly conducts himself in the presence of his superior." Joe took another pull and yawned. "Well, forget about it. With any man who goes into a fracas with me, I like to be on close terms. When things pickle, I want him to be on my side, not nursing some peeve brought on by his officer trying to give him an inferiority complex."

The little man was eying him in surprise.

Joe finished his highball and came to his feet to get another one. He said, "On two occasions I've had an orderly save my life. I'm not taking any chances but that there might be a third opportunity."

"Well, yessir. Does the captain want me to get him—"

"I'll get it," Joe said.

When he'd returned to his chair, he said, "Why did you join up with Baron Haer, Max?"

The other shrugged it off. "The usual. The excitement. The idea of all those fans watching me on Telly. The share of common stock I'll get. And, you never know, maybe a promotion in caste. I wouldn't mind making Upper-Lower."

Joe said sourly, "One fracas and you'll be over that desire to have the buffs watching you on Telly while they sit around in their front rooms sucking on tranks. And you'll probably be over the desire for the excitement, too. Of course, the share of stock is another thing."

"You aren't just countin' down, captain," Max said, an almost surly overtone in his voice. "You don't know what it's like being born with no more common stock shares than a Mid-Lower."

Joe held his peace, sipping at his drink, taking this one more slowly. He let his eyebrows rise to encourage the other to go on.

Max said doggedly, "Sure, they call it People's Capitalism and everybody gets issued enough shares to insure him a basic living all the way from the cradle to the grave, like they say. But let me tell you, you're a Middle and you don't realize how basic the basic living of a Lower can be."

Joe yawned. If he hadn't been so tired, there would have been more amusement in the situation.

Max was still dogged. "Unless you can add to those shares of stock, it's pretty drab, captain. You wouldn't know."

Joe said, "Why don't you work? A Lower can always add to his stock by working."

Max stirred in indignity. "Work? Listen, sir, that's just one more field that's been automated right out of existence. Category Food Preparation, Sub-division Cooking, Branch Chef. Cooking isn't left in the hands of slobs who might drop a cake of soap into the soup. It's done automatic. The only new changes made in cooking are by real top experts, almost scientists like. And most of them are Uppers, mind you."

Joe Mauser sighed inwardly. So his find in batmen wasn't going to be as wonderful as all that, after all. The man might have been born into the food preparation category from a long line of chefs, but evidently he knew precious little about his field. Joe might have suspected. He himself had been born into Clothing Category, Sub-division Shoes, Branch Repair—Cobbler—a meaningless trade since shoes were no longer repaired but discarded upon showing signs of wear. In an economy of complete abundance, there is little reason for repair of basic commodities. It was high time the government investigated category assignment and reshuffled and reassigned half the nation's population. But then, of course, was the question of what to do with the technologically unemployed.

Max was saying, "The only way I could figure on a promotion to a higher caste, or the only way to earn stock shares, was by crossing categories. And you know what that means. Either Category Military, or Category Religion and I sure as Zen don't know nothing about religion."

Joe said mildly, "Theoretically, you can cross categories into any field you want, Max."

Max snorted. "Theoretically is right ... sir. You ever heard about anybody born a Lower, or even a Middle like yourself, cross categories to, say, some Upper category like banking?"

Joe chuckled. He liked this peppery little fellow. If Max worked out as well as Joe thought he might, there was a possibility of taking him along to the next fracas.

Max was saying, "I'm not saying anything against the old time way of doing things or talking against the government, but I'll tell you, captain, every year goes by it gets harder and harder for a man to raise his caste or to earn some additional stock shares."

The applejack had worked enough on Joe for him to rise against one of his pet peeves. He said, "That term, the old time way, is strictly Telly talk, Max. We don't do things *the old time way*. No nation in history ever has — with the possible exception of Egypt. Socio-economics are in a continual flux and here in this country we no more do things in the way they did fifty years ago, than fifty years ago they did them the way the American Revolutionists outlined back in the Eighteenth Century."

Max was staring at him. "I don't get that, sir."

Joe said impatiently, "Max, the politico-economic system we have today is an outgrowth of what went earlier. The welfare state, the freezing of the status quo, the Frigid Fracas between the West-world and the Sov-world, industrial automation until useful employment is all but needless — all these things were to be found in embryo more than fifty years ago."

"Well, maybe the captain's right, but you gotta admit, sir, that mostly we do things the old way. We still got the Constitution and the two-party system and —"

Joe was wearying of the conversation now. You seldom ran into anyone, even in Middle caste, the traditionally professional class, interested enough in such subjects to be worth arguing with. He said, "The Constitution, Max, has got to the point of the Bible. Interpret it the way you wish, and you can find anything. If not, you can always make a new amendment. So far as the two-party system is concerned, what effect does it have when there are no differences between the two parties? That phase of pseudo-democracy was beginning as far back as the 1930s when they began passing State laws hindering the emerging of new political parties. By the time they were insured against a third party working its way through the maze of election laws, the two parties had become so similar that elections became almost as big a farce as over in the Sov-world."

"A farce?" Max ejaculated indignantly, forgetting his servant status. "That means not so good, doesn't it? Far as I'm concerned, election day is tops. The one day a Lower is just as good as an Upper. The one day how many shares you got makes no difference. Everybody has everything."

"Sure, sure, sure," Joe sighed. "The modern equivalent of the Roman Bacchanalia. Election day in the West-world when no one, for just that one day, is freer than anyone else."

"Well, what's wrong with that?" The other was all but belligerent. "That's the trouble with you Middles and Uppers, you don't know how it is to be a Lower and—"

Joe snapped suddenly, "I was born a Mid-Lower myself, Max. Don't give me that nonsense."

Max gaped at him, utterly unbelieving.

Joe's irritation fell away. He held out his glass. "Get us a couple of more drinks, Max, and I'll tell you a story."

By the time the fresh drink came, Joe Mauser was sorry he'd made the offer. He thought back. He hadn't told anyone the Joe Mauser story in many a year. And, as he recalled, the last time had been when he was well into his cups, on an election day at that, and his listener had been a Low-Upper, a hereditary aristocrat, one of the one per cent of the upper strata of the nation. Zen! How the man had laughed. He'd roared his amusement till the tears ran.

However, Joe said, "Max, I was born in the same caste you were—average father, mother, sisters and brothers. They subsisted on the basic income guaranteed from birth, sat and watched Telly for an unbelievable number of hours each day, took trank to keep themselves happy. And thought I was crazy because I didn't. Dad was the sort of man who'd take his belt off to a child of his who questioned such school taught slogans as *What was good enough for Daddy is good enough for me.*

"They were all fracas fans, of course. As far back as I can remember the picture is there of them gathered around the Telly, screaming excitement." Joe Mauser sneered, uncharacteristically.

"You don't sound much like you're in favor of your trade, captain," Max said.

Joe came to his feet, putting down his still half-full glass. "I'll make this epic story short, Max. As you said, the two actually valid methods of rising above the level in which you were born are in the Military and Religious Categories. Like you, even I couldn't stomach the latter."

Joe Mauser hesitated, then finished it off. "Max, there have been few societies that man has evolved that didn't allow in some manner for the competent or sly, the intelligent or the opportunist, the brave or the strong, to work his way to the top. I don't know which of these I personally fit into, but I rebel against remaining in the lower categories of a stratified society. Do I make myself clear?"

"Well, no sir, not exactly."

Joe said flatly, "I'm going to fight my way to the top, and nothing is going to stand in the way. Is that clearer?"

"Yessir," Max said, taken aback.

CHAPTER IV

After routine morning duties, Joe Mauser returned to his billet and mystified Max Mainz by not only changing into mufti himself but having Max do the same.

In fact, the new batman protested faintly. He hadn't nearly, as yet, got over the glory of wearing his kilts and was looking forward to parading around town in them. He had a point, of course. The appointed time for the fracas was getting closer and buffs were beginning to stream into town to bask in the atmosphere of threatened death. Everybody knew what a military center, on the outskirts of a fracas reservation such as the Catskills, was like immediately preceding a clash between rival corporations. The high-strung gaiety, the drinking, the overtranking, the relaxation of mores. Even a Rank Private had it made. Admiring civilians to buy drinks and hang on your every word, and more important still, sensuous-eyed women, their faces slack in thinly suppressed passion. It was a recognized phenomenon, even Max Mainz knew — this desire on the part of women Telly fans to date a man, and then watch him later, killing or being killed.

"Time enough to wear your fancy uniform," Joe Mauser growled at him. "In fact, tomorrow's a local election day. Parlay that up on top of all the fracas fans gravitating into town and you'll have a wingding the likes of nothing you've seen before."

"Well yessir," Max begrudged. "Where're we going now, captain?"

"To the airport. Come along."

Joe Mauser led the way to his sports hovercar and as soon as the two were settled into the bucket seats, hit the lift lever with the butt of his left hand. Aircushion-borne, he trod down on the accelerator.

Max Mainz was impressed. "You know," he said. "I never been in one of these swanky sports jobs before. The kinda car you can afford on the income of a Mid-Lower's stock aren't—"

"Knock it off," Joe said wearily. "Carping we'll always have with us evidently, but in spite of all the beefing in every strata from Low-Lower to Upper-Middle, I've yet to see any signs of organized protest against our present politico-economic system."

"Hey," Max said. "Don't get me wrong. What was good enough for Dad is good enough for me. You won't catch me talking against the government."

"Hm-m-m," Joe murmured. "And all the other cliches taught to us to preserve the status quo, our People's Capitalism." They were reaching the outskirts of town, crossing the Esopus. The airport lay only a mile or so beyond.

It was obviously too deep for Max, and since he didn't understand, he assumed his superior didn't know what he was talking about. He said, tolerantly, "Well, what's wrong with People's Capitalism? Everybody owns the corporations. Damnsight better than the Sovs have."

Joe said sourly. "We've got one optical illusion, they've got another, Max. Over there they claim the proletariat owns the means of production. Great. But the Party members are the ones who control it, and, as a result they manage to do all right for themselves. The Party hierarchy over there are like our Uppers over here."

"Yeah." Max was being particularly dense. "I've seen a lot about it on Telly. You know, when there isn't a good fracas on, you tune to one of them educational shows, like—"

Joe winced at the term *educational*, but held his peace.

"It's pretty rugged over there. But in the West-world, the people own a corporation's stock and they run it and get the benefit."

"At least it makes a beautiful story," Joe said dryly. "Look, Max. Suppose you have a corporation that has two hundred thousand shares out and they're distributed among one hundred thousand and one persons. One hundred thousand of these own one share apiece, but the remaining stockholder owns the other hundred thousand."

"I don't know what you're getting at," Max said.

Joe Mauser was tired of the discussion. "Briefly," he said, "we have the illusion that this is a People's Capitalism, with all stock in the hands of the People. Actually, as ever before, the stock is in the hands of the Uppers, all except a mere dribble. They own the country and they run it for their own benefit."

Max shot a less than military glance at him. "Hey, you're not one of these Sovs yourself, are you?"

They were coming into the parking area near the Administration Building of the airport. "No," Joe said so softly that Max could hardly hear his words. "Only a Mid-Middle on the make."

Followed by Max, he strode quickly to the Administration Building, presented his credit identification at the desk and requested a light aircraft for a period of three hours. The clerk, hardly looking up, began going through motions, speaking into telescreens.

The clerk said finally, "You might have a small wait, sir. Quite a few of the officers involved in this fracas have been renting out taxi-planes almost as fast as they're available."

That didn't surprise Joe Mauser. Any competent officer made a point of an aerial survey of the battle reservation before going into a fracas. Aircraft, of course, couldn't be used *during* the fray, since they postdated the turn of the century, and hence were relegated to the cemetery of military devices along with such items as nuclear weapons, tanks, and even gasoline-propelled vehicles of size to be useful.

Use an aircraft in a fracas, or even *build* an aircraft for military usage and you'd have a howl go up from the military attaches from the Sov-world that would be heard all the way to Budapest. Not a fracas went by but there were scores, if not hundreds, of military observers, keen-eyed to check whether or not any really modern tools of war were being illegally utilized. Joe Mauser sometimes wondered if the West-world observers, over in the Sov-world, were as hair fine in their living up to the rules of the Universal Disarmament Pact. Probably. But, for that matter, they didn't have the same system of fighting fracases over there, as in the West.

Joe took a chair while he waited and thumbed through a fan magazine. From time to time he found his own face in such publications. He was a third-rate celebrity, really. Luck hadn't been with him so far as the buffs were concerned. They wanted spectacular victories, murderous situations in which they could lose themselves in vicarious sadistic thrills. Joe had reached most of his peaks while in retreat, or commanding a holding action. His officers appreciated him and so did the ultra-knowledgeable fracas buffs—but he was all but an unknown to the average dim wit who spent most of his life glued to the Telly set, watching men butcher each other.

On the various occasions when matters had pickled and Joe had to fight his way out against difficult odds, using spectacular tactics in desperation, he was almost always off camera. Purely luck. On top of skill, determination, experience and courage, you had to have luck in the Military Category to get anywhere.

This time Joe was going to manufacture his own.

A voice said, "Ah, Captain Mauser."

Joe looked up, then came to his feet quickly. In automatic reflex, he began to come to the salute but then caught himself. He said stiffly, "My compliments, Marshal Cogswell."

The other was a smallish man, but strikingly strong of face and strongly built. His voice was clipped, clear and had the air of command as though born with it. He, like Joe, wore mufti and now extended his hand to be shaken.

"I hear you've signed up with Baron Haer, captain. I was rather expecting you to come in with me. Had a place for a good aide de camp. Liked your work in that last fracas we went through together."

"Thank you, sir," Joe said. Stonewall Cogswell was as good a tactician as freelanced and he was more than that. He was a judge of men and a stickler for detail. And right now, if Joe Mauser knew Marshal Stonewall Cogswell as well as he thought, Cogswell was smelling a rat. There was no reason why old pro Joe Mauser should sign up with a sure loser like Vacuum Tube when he could have earned more shares taking a commission with Hovercraft.

He was looking at Joe brightly, the question in his eyes. Three or four of his staff were behind a few paces, looking polite, but Cogswell didn't bring them into the conversation. Joe knew most by sight. Good men all. Old pros all. He felt another twinge of doubt.

Joe had to cover. He said, "I was offered a particularly good contract, sir. Too good to resist."

The other nodded, as though inwardly coming to a satisfactory conclusion. "Baron Haer's connections, eh? He's probably offered to back you for a bounce in caste. Is that it, Joe?"

Joe Mauser flushed. Stonewall Cogswell knew what he was talking about. He'd been born into Middle status himself and had become an Upper the hard way. His path wasn't as long as Joe's was going to be, but long enough and he knew how rocky the climb was. How very rocky.

Joe said, stiffly, "I'm afraid I'm in no position to discuss my commander's military contracts, marshal. We're in mufti, but after all —"

Cogswell's lean face registered one of his infrequent grimaces of humor. "I understand, Joe. Well, good luck and I hope things don't pickle for you in the coming fracas. Possibly we'll find ourselves aligned together again at some future time."

"Thank you, sir," Joe said, once more having to catch himself to prevent an automatic salute.

Cogswell and his staff went off, leaving Joe looking after them. Even the marshal's staff members were top men, any of whom could have conducted a divisional magnitude fracas. Joe felt the coldness in his stomach again. Although it must have looked like a cinch, the enemy wasn't taking any chances whatsoever. Cogswell and his officers were undoubtedly here at the airport for the same reason as Joe. They wanted a thorough aerial reconnaissance of the battlefield-to-be, before the issue was joined.

Max was standing at his elbow. "Who was that, sir? Looks like a real tough one."

"He is a real tough one," Joe said sourly. "That's Stonewall Cogswell, the best field commander in North America."

Max pursed his lips. "I never seen him out of uniform before. Lots of times on Telly, but never out of uniform. I thought he was taller than that."

"He fights with his brains," Joe said, still looking after the craggy field marshal. "He doesn't have to be any taller."

Max scowled. "Where'd he ever get that nickname, sir?"

"Stonewall?" Joe was turning to resume his chair and magazine. "He's supposed to be a student of a top general back in the American Civil War. Uses some of the original Stonewall's tactics."

Max was out of his depth. "American Civil War? Was that much of a fracas, captain? It musta been before my time."

"It was quite a fracas," Joe said dryly. "Lot of good lads died. A hundred years after it was fought, the *reasons* it was fought seemed about as valid as those we fight fracases for today. Personally I—"

He had to cut it short. They were calling him on the address system. His aircraft was ready. Joe made his way to the hangars, followed by Max Mainz. He was going to pilot the airplane himself and old Stonewall Cogswell would have been surprised at what Joe Mauser was looking for.

CHAPTER V

By the time they had returned to quarters, there was a message waiting for Captain Mauser. He was to report to the officer commanding reconnaissance.

Joe redressed in the Haer kilts and proceeded to headquarters.

The officer commanding reconnaissance turned out to be none other than Balt Haer, natty as ever, and, as ever, arrogantly tapping his swagger stick against his leg.

"Zen! Captain," he complained. "Where have you been? Off on a trank kick? We've got to get organized."

Joe Mauser snapped him a salute. "No, sir. I rented an aircraft to scout out the terrain over which we'll be fighting."

"Indeed. And what were your impressions, captain?" There was an overtone which suggested that it made little difference what impressions a captain of cavalry might have gained.

Joe shrugged. "Largely mountains, hills, woods. Good reconnaissance is going to make the difference in this one. And in the fracas itself cavalry is going to be more important than either artillery or infantry. A Nathan Forrest fracas, sir. A matter of getting there fustest with the mostest."

Balt Haer said amusedly. "Thanks for your opinion, captain. Fortunately, our staff has already come largely to the same conclusions. Undoubtedly, they'll be glad to hear your wide experience bears them out."

Joe said evenly, "It's a rather obvious conclusion, of course." He took this as it came, having been through it before. The dilettante amateur's dislike of the old pro. The amateur in command who knew full well he was less capable than many of those below him in rank.

"Of course, captain," Balt Haer flicked his swagger stick against his leg. "But to the point. Your squadron is to be deployed as scouts under my overall command. You've had cavalry experience, I assume."

"Yes, sir. In various fracases over the past fifteen years."

"Very well. Now then, to get to the reason I have summoned you. Yesterday in my father's office you intimated that you had some grandiose scheme which would bring victory to the Haer colors. But then, on some thin excuse, refused to divulge just what the scheme might be."

Joe Mauser looked at him unblinkingly.

Balt Haer said: "Now I'd like to have your opinion on just how Vacuum Tube Transport can extract itself from what would seem a poor position at best."

In all there were four others in the office, two women clerks fluttering away at typers, and two of Balt Haer's junior officers. They seemed only mildly interested in the conversation between Balt and Joe.

Joe wet his lips carefully. The Haer scion was his commanding officer. He said, "Sir, what I had in mind is a new gimmick. At this stage, if I told anybody and it leaked, it'd never be effective, not even this first time."

Haer observed him coldly. "And you think me incapable of keeping your secret, ah, *gimmick*, I believe is the idiomatic term you used."

Joe Mauser's eyes shifted around the room, taking in the other four, who were now looking at him.

Bait Haer rapped, "These members of my staff are all trusted Haer employees, Captain Mauser. They are not fly-by-night freelancers hired for a week or two."

Joe said, "Yes, sir. But it's been my experience that one person can hold a secret. It's twice as hard for two, and from there on it's a decreasing probability in a geometric ratio."

The younger Haer's stick rapped the side of his leg, impatiently. "Suppose I inform you that this is a command, captain? I have little confidence in a supposed gimmick that will rescue our forces from disaster and I rather dislike the idea of a captain of one of my squadrons dashing about with such a bee in his bonnet when he should be obeying my commands."

Joe kept his voice respectful. "Then, sir, I'd request that we take the matter to the Commander in Chief, your father."

"Indeed!"

Joe said, "Sir, I've been working on this a long time. I can't afford to risk throwing the idea away."

Bait Haer glared at him. "Very well, captain. I'll call your bluff, come along." He turned on his heel and headed from the room.

Joe Mauser shrugged in resignation and followed him.

The old Baron wasn't much happier about Joe Mauser's secrets than was his son. It had only been the day before that he had taken Joe on, but already he had seemed to have aged in appearance. Evidently, each hour that went by made it increasingly clear just how perilous a position he had assumed. Vacuum Tube Transport had elbowed, buffaloed, bluffed and edged itself up to the outskirts of the really big time. The Baron's ability, his aggressiveness, his flair, his political pull, had all helped, but now the chips were down. He was up against one of the biggies, and this particular biggy was tired of ambitious little Vacuum Tube Transport.

He listened to his son's words, listened to Joe's defense.

He said, looking at Joe, "If I understand this, you have some scheme which you think will bring victory in spite of what seems a disastrous situation."

"Yes, sir."

The two Haers looked at him, one impatiently, the other in weariness.

Joe said, "I'm gambling everything on this, sir. I'm no Rank Private in his first fracas. I deserve to be given some leeway."

Balt Haer snorted. "Gambling everything! What in Zen would *you* have to gamble, captain? The whole Haer family fortunes are tied up. Hovercraft is out for blood. They won't be satisfied with a token victory and a negotiated compromise. They'll devastate us. Thousands of mercenaries killed, with all that means in indemnities; millions upon million in expensive military equipment, most of which we've had to hire and will have to recompensate for. Can you imagine the value of our stock after Stonewall Cogswell has finished with us? Why, every two by four trucking outfit in North America will be challenging us, and we won't have the forces to meet a minor skirmish."

Joe reached into an inner pocket and laid a sheaf of documents on the desk of Baron Malcolm Haer. The Baron scowled down at them.

Joe said simply, "I've been accumulating stock since before I was eighteen and I've taken good care of my portfolio in spite of taxes and the various other pitfalls which make the accumulation of capital practically impossible. Yesterday, I sold all of my portfolio I was legally allowed to sell and converted to Vacuum Tube Transport." He added, dryly, "Getting it at an excellent rate, by the way."

Balt Haer mulled through the papers, unbelievingly. "Zen!" he ejaculated. "The fool really did it. He's sunk a small fortune into our stock."

Baron Haer growled at his son, "You seem considerably more convinced of our defeat than the captain, here. Perhaps I should reverse your positions of command."

His son grunted, but said nothing.

Old Malcolm Haer's eyes came back to Joe. "Admittedly, I thought you on the romantic side yesterday, with your hints of some scheme which would lead us out of the wilderness, so to speak. Now I wonder if you might not really have something. Very well, I respect your claimed need for secrecy. Espionage is not exactly an antiquated military field."

"Thank you, sir."

But the Baron was still staring at him. "However, there's more to it than that. Why not take this great scheme to Marshal Cogswell? And yesterday you mentioned that the Telly sets of the nation would be tuned in on this fracas, and obviously you are correct. The question becomes, what of it?"

The fat was in the fire now. Joe Mauser avoided the haughty stare of young Balt Haer and addressed himself to the older man. "You have political pull, sir. Oh, I know you don't make and break presidents. You couldn't even pull enough wires to keep Hovercraft from making this a divisional magnitude fracas — but you have pull enough for my needs."

Baron Haer leaned back in his chair, his barrel-like body causing that article of furniture to creak. He crossed his hands over his stomach. "And what are your needs, Captain Mauser?"

Joe said evenly, "If I can bring this off, I'll be a fracas buff celebrity. I don't have any illusions about the fickleness of the Telly fans, but for a day or two I'll be on top. If at the same time I had your all out support, pulling what strings you could reach — "

"Why then, you'd be promoted to Upper, wouldn't you, captain?" Balt Haer finished for him, amusement in his voice.

"That's what I'm gambling on," Joe said evenly.

The younger Haer grinned at his father superciliously. "So our captain says he will defeat Stonewall Cogswell in return for you sponsoring his becoming a member of the nation's elite."

"Good Heavens, is the supposed cream of the nation now selected on no higher a level than this?" There was sarcasm in the words.

The three men turned. It was the girl Joe had bumped into the day before. The Haers didn't seem surprised at her entrance.

"Nadine," the older man growled. "Captain Joseph Mauser who has been given a commission in our forces."

Joe went through the routine of a Middle of officer's rank being introduced to a lady of Upper caste. She smiled at him, somewhat mockingly, and failed to make standard response.

Nadine Haer said, "I repeat, what is this service the captain can render the house of Haer so important that pressure should be brought to raise him to Upper caste? It would seem unlikely that he is a noted scientist, an outstanding artist, a great teacher—"

Joe said, uncomfortably, "They say the military is a science, too."

Her expression was almost as haughty as that of her brother. "Do they? I have never thought so."

"Really, Nadine," her father grumbled. "This is hardly your affair."

"No? In a few days I shall be repairing the damage you have allowed, indeed sponsored, to be committed upon the bodies of possibly thousands of now healthy human beings."

Balt said nastily, "Nobody asked you to join the medical staff, Nadine. You could have stayed in your laboratory, figuring out new methods of preventing the human race from replenishing itself."

The girl was obviously not the type to redden, but her anger was manifest. She spun on her brother. "If the race continues its present maniac course, possibly more effective methods of birth control *are* the most important development we could make. Even to the ultimate discovery of preventing all future conception."

Joe caught himself in mid-chuckle.

But not in time. She spun on him in his turn. "Look at yourself in that silly skirt. A professional soldier! A killer! In my opinion the most useless occupation ever devised by man. Parasite on the best and useful members of society. Destroyer by trade!"

Joe began to open his mouth, but she overrode him. "Yes, yes. I know. I've read all the nonsense that has accumulated down through the ages about the need for, the glory of, the sacrifice of the professional soldier. How they defend their country. How they give all for the common good. Zen! What nonsense."

Balt Haer was smirking sourly at her. "The theory today is, Nadine, old thing, that professionals such as the captain are gathering experience in case a serious fracas with the Sovs ever develops. Meanwhile his training is kept at a fine edge fighting in our inter-corporation, inter-union, or union-corporation fracases that develop in our private enterprise society."

She laughed her scorn. "And what a theory! Limited to the weapons which prevailed before 1900. If there was ever real conflict between the Sov-world and our own, does anyone really believe either would stick to such arms? Why, aircraft, armored vehicles, yes, and nuclear weapons and rockets, would be in overnight use."

Joe was fascinated by her furious attack. He said, "Then, what would you say was the purpose of the fracases, Miss—"

"Circuses," she snorted. "The old Roman games, all over again, and a hundred times worse. Blood and guts sadism. The quest of a frustrated person for satisfaction in another's pain. Our Lowers of today are as useless and frustrated as the Roman proletariat and potentially they're just as dangerous as the mob that once dominated Rome. Automation, the second industrial revolution, has eliminated for all practical purposes the need for their labor. So we give them bread and circuses. And every year that goes by the circuses must be increasingly sadistic, death on an increasing scale, or they aren't satisfied. Once it was enough to have fictional mayhem, cowboys and Indians, gangsters, or G.I.s versus the Nazis, Japs or Commies, but that's passed. Now we need *real* blood and guts."

Baron Haer snapped finally, "All right, Nadine. We've heard this lecture before. I doubt if the captain is interested, particularly since you don't seem to be able to get beyond the protesting stage and have yet to come up with an answer."

"I have an answer!"

"Ah?" Balt Haer raised his eyebrows, mockingly.

"Yes! Overthrow this silly status society. Resume the road to progress. Put our people to useful endeavor, instead of sitting in front of their Telly sets, taking trank pills to put them in a happy daze and watching sadistic fracases to keep them in thrills, and their minds from their condition."

Joe had figured on keeping out of the controversy with this firebrand, but now, really interested, he said, "Progress to where?"

She must have caught in his tone that he wasn't needling. She frowned at him. "I don't know man's goal, if there is one. I'm not even sure it's important. It's the road that counts. The endeavor. The dream. The effort expended to make a world a better place than it was at the time of your birth."

Balt Haer said mockingly, "That's the trouble with you, Sis. Here we've reached Utopia and you don't admit it."

"Utopia!"

"Certainly. Take a poll. You'll find nineteen people out of twenty happy with things just the way they are. They have full tummies and security, lots of leisure and trank pills to make matters seem even rosier than they are—and they're rather rosy already."

"Then what's the necessity of this endless succession of bloody fracases, covered to the most minute bloody detail on the Telly?"

Baron Haer cut things short. "We've hashed and rehashed this before, Nadine and now we're too busy to debate further." He turned to Joe Mauser.

"Very well, captain, you have my pledge. I wish I felt as optimistic as you seem to be about your prospects. That will be all for now, captain."

Joe saluted and executed an about face.

In the outer offices, when he had closed the door behind him, he rolled his eyes upward in mute thanks to whatever powers might be. He had somehow gained the enmity of Balt, his immediate superior, but he'd also gained the support of Baron Haer himself, which counted considerably more.

He considered for a moment, Nadine Haer's words. She was obviously a malcontent, but, on the other hand, her opinions of his chosen profession weren't too different than his own. However, given this victory, this upgrading in caste, and Joe Mauser would be in a position to retire.

The door opened and shut behind him and he half turned.

Nadine Haer, evidently still caught up in the hot words between herself and her relatives, glared at him. All of which stressed the beauty he had noticed the day before. She was an almost unbelievably pretty girl, particularly when flushed with anger.

It occurred to him with a blowlike suddenness that, if his caste was raised to Upper, he would be in a position to woo such as Nadine Haer.

He looked into her furious face and said, "I was intrigued, Miss Haer, with what you had to say, and I'd like to discuss some of your points. I wonder if I could have the pleasure of your company at some nearby refreshment—"

"My, how formal an invitation, captain. I suppose you had in mind sitting and flipping back a few trank pills."

Joe looked at her. "I don't believe I've had a trank in the past twenty years, Miss Haer. Even as a boy, I didn't particularly take to having my senses dulled with drug-induced pleasure."

Some of her fury was abating, but she was still critical of the professional mercenary. Her eyes went up and down his uniform in scorn. "You seem to make pretenses of being cultivated, captain. Then why your chosen profession?"

He'd had the answer to that for long years. He said now, simply, "I told you I was born a Lower. Given that, little counts until I fight my way out of it. Had I been born in a feudalist society, I would have attempted to batter myself into the nobility. Under classical capitalism, I would have done my utmost to accumulate a fortune, enough to reach an effective position in society. Now, under People's Capitalism ..."

She snorted, "Industrial Feudalism would be the better term."

"... I realize I can't even start to fulfill myself until I am a member of the Upper caste."

Her eyes had narrowed, and the anger was largely gone. "But you chose the military field in which to better yourself?"

"Government propaganda to the contrary, it is practically impossible to raise yourself in other fields. I didn't build this world, possibly I don't even approve of it, but since I'm in it I have no recourse but to follow its rules."

Her eyebrows arched. "Why not try to change the rules?"

Joe blinked at her.

Nadine Haer said, "Let's look up that refreshment you were talking about. In fact, there's a small coffee bar around the corner where it'd be possible for one of Baron Haer's brood to have a cup with one of her father's officers of Middle caste."

CHAPTER VI

The following morning, hands on the pillow beneath his head, Joe Mauser stared up at the ceiling of his room and rehashed his session with Nadine Haer. It hadn't taken him five minutes to come to the conclusion that he was in love with the girl, but it had taken him the rest of the evening to keep himself under rein and not let the fact get through to her.

He wanted to talk about the way her mouth tucked in at the corners, but she was hot on the evolution of society. He would have liked to have kissed that impossibly perfectly shaped ear of hers, but she was all for exploring the reasons why man had reached his present impasse. Joe was for holding hands, and staring into each other's eyes, she was for delving into the differences between the West-world and the Sov-world and the possibility of resolving them.

Of course, to keep her company at all it had been necessary to suppress his own desires and to go along. It obviously had never occurred to her that a Middle might have romantic ideas involving Nadine Haer. It had simply not occurred to her, no matter the radical teachings she advocated.

Most of their world was predictable from what had gone before. In spite of popular fable to the contrary, the division between classes had become increasingly clear. Among other things, tax systems were such that it became all but impossible for a citizen born poor to accumulate a fortune. Through ability he might rise to the point of earning fabulous sums—and wind up in debt to the tax collector. A great inventor, a great artist, had little chance of breaking into the domain of what finally became the small percentage of the population now known as Uppers. Then, too, the rising cost of a really good education became such that few other than those born into the Middle or Upper castes could afford the best of schools. Castes tended to perpetuate themselves.

Politically, the nation had fallen increasingly deeper into the two-party system, both parties of which were tightly controlled by the same group of Uppers. Elections had become a farce, a great national holiday in which stereotyped patriotic speeches, pretenses of unity between all castes, picnics, beer busts and trank binges predominated for one day.

Economically, too, the augurs had been there. Production of the basics had become so profuse that poverty in the old sense of the word had become nonsensical. There was an abundance of the necessities of life for all. Social security, socialized medicine, unending unemployment insurance, old age pensions, pensions for veterans, for widows and children, for the unfit, pensions and doles for this, that and the other, had doubled, and doubled again, until everyone had security for life. The Uppers, true enough, had opulence far beyond that known by the Middles and lived like Gods compared to the Lowers. But all had security. They had agreed, thus far, Joe and Nadine. But then had come debate.

"Then why," Joe had asked her, "haven't we achieved what your brother called it? Why isn't this Utopia? Isn't it what man has been yearning for, down through the ages? Where did the wheel come off? What happened to the dream?"

Nadine had frowned at him—beautifully, he thought. "It's not the first time man has found abundance in a society, though never to this degree. The Incas had it, for instance."

"I don't know much about them," Joe admitted. "An early form of communism with a sort of military-priesthood at the top."

She had nodded, her face serious, as always. "And for themselves, the Romans more or less had it—at the expense of the nations they conquered, of course."

"And—" Joe prodded.

"And in these examples the same thing developed. Society ossified. Joe," she said, using his first name for the first time, and in a manner that set off a new count down in his blood, "a ruling caste and a socio-economic system perpetuates itself, just so long as it ever can. No matter what damage it may do to society as a whole, it perpetuates itself even to the point of complete destruction of everything.

"Remember Hitler? Adolf the Aryan and his Thousand Year Reich? When it became obvious he had failed, and the only thing that could result from continued resistance would be destruction of Germany's cities and millions of her people, did he and his clique resign or surrender? Certainly not. They attempted to bring down the whole German structure in a Götterdammerung."

Nadine Haer was deep into her theme, her eyes flashing her conviction. "A socio-economic system reacts like a living organism. It attempts to live on, indefinitely, agonizingly, no matter how antiquated it might have become. The Roman politico-economic system continued for centuries after it should have been replaced. Such reformers as the Gracchus brothers were assassinated or thrust aside so that the entrenched elements could perpetuate themselves, and when Rome finally fell, darkness descended for a thousand years on Western progress."

Joe had never gone this far in his thoughts. He said now, somewhat uncomfortably, "Well, what would replace what we have now? If you took power from you Uppers, who could direct the country? The Lowers? That's not even funny. Take away their fracases and their trank pills and they'd go berserk. They don't *want* anything else."

Her mouth worked. "Admittedly, we've already allowed things to deteriorate much too far. We should have done something long ago. I'm not sure I know the answer. All I know is that in order to maintain the status quo, we're not utilizing the efforts of more than a fraction of our people. Nine out of ten of us spend our lives sitting before the Telly, sucking tranks. Meanwhile, the motivation for continued progress seems to have withered away. Our Upper political circles are afraid some seemingly minor change might avalanche, so more and more we lean upon the old way of doing things."

Joe had put up mild argument. "I've heard the case made that the Lowers are fools and the reason our present socio-economic system makes it so difficult to rise from Lower to Upper is that you cannot make a fool understand he is one. You can only make him angry. If some, who are not fools, are allowed to advance from Lower to Upper, the vast mass who are fools will be angry because they are not allowed to. That's why the Military Category is made a channel of advance. To take that road, a man gives up his security and he'll die if he's a fool."

Nadine had been scornful. "That reminds me of the old contention by racial segregationalists that the Negroes *smelled* bad. First they put them in a position where they had insufficient bathing facilities, their diet inadequate, and their teeth uncared for, and then protested that they couldn't be associated with because of their odor. Today, we are born within our castes. If an Upper is inadequate, he nevertheless remains an Upper. An accident of birth makes him an aristocrat; environment, family, training, education, friends, traditions and laws maintain him in that position. But a Lower who potentially has the greatest of value to society, is born handicapped and he's hard put not to wind up before a Telly, in a mental daze from trank. Sure he's a fool, he's never been *allowed* to develop himself."

Yes, Joe reflected now, it had been quite an evening. In a life of more than thirty years devoted to rebellion, he had never met anyone so outspoken as Nadine Haer, nor one who had thought it through as far as she had.

He grunted. His own revolt was against the level at which he had found himself in society, not the structure of society itself. His whole *raison d'être* was to lift himself to Upper status. It came as a shock to him to find a person he admired who had been born into Upper caste, desirous of tearing the whole system down.

His thoughts were interrupted by the door opening and the face of Max Mainz grinning in at him. Joe was mildly surprised at his orderly not knocking before opening the door. Max evidently had a lot to learn.

The little man blurted, "Come on, Joe. Let's go out on the town!"

"*Joe?*" Joe Mauser raised himself to one elbow and stared at the other. "Leaving aside the merits of your suggestion for the moment, do you think you should address an officer by his first name?"

Max Mainz came fully into the bedroom, his grin still wider. "You forgot! It's election day!"

"Oh." Joe Mauser relaxed into his pillow. "So it is. No duty for today, eh?"

"No duty for anybody," Max crowed. "What'd you say we go into town and have a few drinks in one of the Upper bars?"

Joe grunted, but began to arise. "What'll that accomplish? On election day, most of the Uppers get done up in their oldest clothes and go slumming down in the Lower quarters."

Max wasn't to be put off so easily. "Well, wherever we go, let's get going. Zen! I'll bet this town is full of fracas buffs from as far as Philly. And on election day, to boot. Wouldn't it be something if I found me a real fracas fan, some Upper-Upper dame?"

Joe laughed at him, even as he headed for the bathroom. As a matter of fact, he rather liked the idea of going into town for the show. "Max," he said over his shoulder, "you're in for a big disappointment. They're all the same. Upper, Lower, or Middle."

"Yeah?" Max grinned back at him. "Well, I'd like the pleasure of finding out if that's true by personal experience."

CHAPTER VII

In a far away past, Kingston had once been the capital of the United States. For a short time, when Washington's men were in flight after the debacle of their defeat in New York City, the government of the United Colonies had held session in this Hudson River town. It had been its one moment of historic glory, and afterward Kingston had slipped back into being a minor city on the edge of the Catskills, approximately halfway between New York and Albany.

Of most recent years, it had become one of the two recruiting centers which bordered the Catskill Military Reservation, which in turn was one of the score or so population cleared areas throughout the continent where rival corporations or unions could meet and settle their differences in combat—given permission of the Military Category Department of the government. And permission was becoming ever easier to acquire.

It had slowly evolved, the resorting to trial by combat to settle disputes between competing corporations, disputes between corporations and unions, disputes between unions over jurisdiction. Slowly, but predictably. Since the earliest days of the first industrial revolution, conflict between these elements had often broken into violence, sometimes on a scale comparable to minor warfare. An early example was the union organizing in Colorado when armed elements of the Western Federation of Miners shot it out with similarly armed "detectives" hired by the mine owners, and later with the troops of an unsympathetic State government.

By the middle of the Twentieth-Century, unions had become one of the biggest businesses in the country, and by this time a considerable amount of the industrial conflict had shifted to fights between them for jurisdiction over dues-paying members. Battles on the waterfront, assassination and counter-assassination by gun-toting goon squads dominated by gangsters, industrial sabotage, frays between pickets and scabs—all were common occurrences.

But it was the coming of Telly which increasingly brought such conflicts literally before the public eye. Zealous reporters made ever greater effort to bring the actual mayhem before the eyes of their viewers, and never were their efforts more highly rewarded.

A society based upon private endeavor is as jealous of a vacuum as is Mother Nature. Give a desire that can be filled profitably, and the means can somehow be found to realize it.

At one point in the nation's history, the railroad lords had dominated the economy, later it became the petroleum princes of Texas and elsewhere, but toward the end of the Twentieth Century the communications industries slowly gained prominence. Nothing was more greatly in demand than feeding the insatiable maw of the Telly fan, nothing, ultimately, became more profitable.

And increasingly, the Telly buff endorsed the more sadistic of the fictional and nonfictional programs presented him. Even in the earliest years of the industry, producers had found that murder and mayhem, war and frontier gunfights, took precedence over less gruesome subjects. Music was drowned out by gunfire, the dance replaced by the shuffle of cowboy and rustler advancing down a dusty street toward each other, their fingertips brushing the grips of their six-shooters, the comedian's banter fell away before the chatter of the gangster's tommy gun.

And increasing realism was demanded. The Telly reporter on the scene of a police arrest, preferably a murder, a rumble between rival gangs of juvenile delinquents, a longshoreman's fray in which scores of workers were hospitalized. When attempts were made to suppress such broadcasts, the howl of freedom of speech and the press went up, financed by tycoons clever enough to realize the value of the subjects they covered so adequately.

The vacuum was there, the desire, the *need*. Bread the populace had. Trank was available to all. But the need was for the circus, the vicious, sadistic circus, and bit by bit, over the years and decades, the way was found to circumvent the country's laws and traditions to supply the need.

Aye, a way is always found. The final Universal Disarmament Pact which had totally banned all weapons invented since the year 1900 and provided for complete inspection, had not ended the fear of war. And thus there was excuse to give the would-be soldier, the potential defender of the country in some future inter-nation conflict, practical experience.

Slowly tolerance grew to allow union and corporation to fight it out, hiring the services of mercenaries. Slowly rules grew up to govern such fracases. Slowly a department of government evolved. The Military Category became as acceptable as the next, and the mercenary a valued, even idolized, member of society. And the field became practically the only one in which a status quo orientated socio-economic system allowed for advancement in caste.

Joe Mauser and Max Mainz strolled the streets of Kingston in an extreme of atmosphere seldom to be enjoyed. Not only was the advent of a divisional magnitude fracas only a short period away, but the freedom of an election day as well. The carnival, the Mardi Gras, the fete, the fiesta, of an election. Election Day, when each aristocrat became only a man, and each man an aristocrat, free of all society's artificially conceived, caste-perpetuating rituals and taboos.

Carnival! The day was young, but already the streets were thick with revelers, with dancers, with drunks. A score of bands played, youngsters in particular ran about attired in costume, there were barbeques and flowing beer kegs. On the outskirts of town were roller coasters and ferris wheels, fun houses and drive-it-yourself miniature cars. Carnival!

Max said happily, "You drink, Joe? Or maybe you like trank, better." Obviously, he loved to roll the other's first name over his tongue.

Joe wondered in amusement how often the little man had found occasion to call a Mid-Middle by his first name. "No trank," he said. "Alcohol for me. Mankind's old faithful."

"Well," Max debated, "get high on alcohol and bingo, a hangover in the morning. But trank? You wake up with a smile."

"And a desire for more trank to keep the mood going," Joe said wryly. "Get smashed on alcohol and you suffer for it eventually."

"Well, that's one way of looking at it," Max argued happily. "So let's start off with a couple of quick ones in this here Upper joint."

Joe looked the place over. He didn't know Kingston overly well, but by the appearance of the building and by the entry, it was probably the swankiest hotel in town. He shrugged. So far as he was concerned, he appreciated the greater comfort and the better service of his Middle caste bars, restaurants and hotels over the ones he had patronized when a Lower. However, his wasn't an immediate desire to push into the preserves of the Uppers; not until he had won rightfully to their status.

But on this occasion the little fellow wanted to drink at an Upper bar. Very well, it was election day. "Let's go," he said to Max.

In the uniform of a Rank Captain of the Military Category, there was little to indicate caste level, and ordinarily given the correct air of nonchalance, Joe Mauser, in uniform, would have been able to go anywhere, without so much as a raised eyebrow—until he had presented his credit card, which indicated his caste. But Max was another thing. He was obviously a Lower, and probably a Low-Lower at that.

But space was made for them at a bar packed with election day celebrants, politicians involved in the day's speeches and voting, higher ranking officers of the Haer forces, having a day off, and various Uppers of both sexes in town for the excitement of the fracas to come.

"Beer," Joe said to the bartender.

"Not me," Max crowed. "Champagne. Only the best for Max Mainz. Give me some of that champagne liquor I always been hearing about."

Joe had the bill credited to his card, and they took their bottles and glasses to a newly abandoned table. The place was too packed to have awaited the services of a waiter, although poor Max probably would have loved such attention. Lower, and even Middle bars and restaurants were universally automated, and the waiter or waitress a thing of yesteryear.

Max looked about the room in awe. "This is living," he announced. "I wonder what they'd say if I went to the desk and ordered a room."

Joe Mauser wasn't as highly impressed as his batman. In fact, he'd often stayed in the larger cities, in hostelries as sumptuous as this, though only of Middle status. Kingston's best was on the mediocre side. He said, "They'd probably tell you they were filled up."

Max was indignant. "Because I'm a Lower? It's *election* day."

Joe said mildly, "Because they probably are filled up. But for that matter, they might brush you off. It's not as though an Upper went to a Middle or Lower hotel and asked for accommodations. But what do you want, justice?"

Max dropped it. He looked down into his glass. "Hey," he complained, "what'd they give me? This stuff tastes like weak hard cider."

Joe laughed. "What did you think it was going to taste like?"

Max took another unhappy sip. "I thought it was supposed to be the best drink you could buy. You know, really strong. It's just bubbly wine."

A voice said, dryly, "Your companion doesn't seem to be a connoisseur of the French vintages, captain."

Joe turned. Balt Haer and two others occupied the table next to them.

Joe chuckled amiably and said, "Truthfully, it was my own reaction, the first time I drank sparkling wine, sir."

"Indeed," Haer said. "I can imagine." He fluttered a hand. "Lieutenant Colonel Paul Warren of Marshal Cogswell's staff, and Colonel Lajos Arpàd, of Budapest—Captain Joseph Mauser."

Joe Mauser came to his feet and clicked his heels, bowing from the waist in approved military protocol. The other two didn't bother to come to their feet, but did condescend to shake hands.

The Sov officer said, disinterestedly, "Ah yes, this is one of your fabulous customs, isn't it? On an election day, everyone is quite entitled to go anywhere. Anywhere at all. And, ah" — he made a sound somewhat like a giggle — "associate with anyone at all."

Joe Mauser resumed his seat then looked at him. "That is correct. A custom going back to the early history of the country when all men were considered equal in such matters as law and civil rights. Gentlemen, may I present Rank Private Max Mainz, my orderly."

Balt Haer, who had obviously already had a few, looked at him dourly. "You can carry these things to the point of the ludicrous, captain. For a man with your ambitions, I'm surprised."

The infantry officer the younger Haer had introduced as Lieutenant Colonel Warren, of Stonewall Cogswell's staff, said idly, "Ambitions? Does the captain have ambitions? How in Zen can a Middle have ambitions, Balt?" He stared at Joe Mauser superciliously, but then scowled. "Haven't I seen you somewhere before?"

Joe said evenly, "Yes, sir. Five years ago we were both with the marshal in a fracas on the Little Big Horn reservation. Your company was pinned down on a knoll by a battery of field artillery. The Marshal sent me to your relief. We sneaked in, up an arroyo, and were able to get most of you out."

"I was wounded," the colonel said, the superciliousness gone and a strange element in his voice above the alcohol there earlier.

Joe Mauser said nothing to that. Max Mainz was stirring unhappily now. These officers were talking above his head, even as they ignored him. He had a vague feeling that he was being defended by Captain Mauser, but he didn't know how, or why.

Balt Haer had been occupied in shouting fresh drinks. Now he turned back to the table. "Well, colonel, it's all very secret, these ambitions of Captain Mauser. I understand he's been an aide de camp to Marshal Cogswell in the past, but the marshal will be distressed to learn that on this occasion Captain Mauser has a secret by which he expects to rout your forces. Indeed, yes, the captain is quite the strategist." Balt Haer laughed abruptly. "And what good will this do the captain? Why on my father's word, if he succeeds, all efforts will be made to make the captain a caste equal of ours. Not just on election day, mind you, but all three hundred sixty-five days of the year."

Joe Mauser was on his feet, his face expressionless. He said, "Shall we go, Max? Gentlemen, it's been a pleasure. Colonel Arpàd, a privilege to meet you. Colonel Warren, a pleasure to renew acquaintance." Joe Mauser turned and, trailed by his orderly, left.

Lieutenant Colonel Warren, pale, was on his feet too.

Balt Haer was chuckling. "Sit down, Paul. Sit down. Not important enough to be angry about. The man's a clod."

Warren looked at him bleakly. "I wasn't angry, Balt. The last time I saw Captain Mauser I was slung over his shoulder. He carried, tugged and dragged me some two miles through enemy fire."

Balt Haer carried it off with a shrug. "Well, that's his profession. Category Military. A mercenary for hire. I assume he received his pay."

"He could have left me. Common sense dictated that he leave me."

Balt Haer was annoyed. "Well, then we see what I've contended all along. The ambitious captain doesn't have common sense."

Colonel Paul Warren shook his head. "You're wrong there. Common sense Joseph Mauser has. Considerable ability, he has. He's one of the best combat men in the field. But I'd hate to serve under him."

The Hungarian was interested. "But why?"

"Because he doesn't have luck, and in the dill you need luck." Warren grunted in sour memory. "Had the Telly cameras been focused on Joe Mauser, there at the Little Big Horn, he would have been a month long sensation to the Telly buffs, with all that means." He grunted again. "There wasn't a Telly team within a mile."

"The captain probably didn't realize that," Balt Haer snorted. "Otherwise his heroics would have been modified."

Warren flushed his displeasure and sat down. He said, "Possibly we should discuss the business before us. If your father is in agreement, the fracas can begin in three days." He turned to the representative of the Sov-world. "You have satisfied yourselves that neither force is violating the Disarmament Pact?"

Lajos Arpàd nodded. "We will wish to have observers on the field, itself, of course. But preliminary observation has been satisfactory." He had been interested in the play between these two and the lower caste officer. He said now, "Pardon me. As you know, this is my first visit to the, uh *West*. I am fascinated. If I understand what just transpired, our Captain Mauser is a capable junior officer ambitious to rise in rank and status in your society." He looked at Balt Haer. "Why are you opposed to his so rising?"

Young Haer was testy about the whole matter. "Of what purpose is an Upper caste if every Tom, Dick and Harry enters it at will?"

Warren looked at the door through which Joe and Max had exited from the cocktail lounge. He opened his mouth to say something, closed it again, and held his peace.

The Hungarian said, looking from one of them to the other, "In the Sov-world we seek out such ambitious persons and utilize their abilities."

Lieutenant Colonel Warren laughed abruptly. "So do we here *theoretically*. We are *free*, whatever that means. However," he added sarcastically, "it does help to have good schooling, good connections, relatives in positions of prominence, abundant shares of good stocks, that sort of thing. And these one is born with, in this free world of ours, Colonel Arpàd."

The Sov military observer clucked his tongue. "An indication of a declining society."

Balt Haer turned on him. "And is it any different in your world?" he said sneeringly. "Is it merely coincidence that the best positions in the Sov-world are held by Party members, and that it is all but impossible for anyone not born of Party member parents to become one? Are not the best schools filled with the children of Party members? Are not only Party members allowed to keep servants? And isn't it so that—"

Lieutenant Colonel Warren said, "Gentlemen, let us not start World War Three at this spot, at this late occasion."

CHAPTER VIII

Baron Malcolm Haer's field headquarters were in the ruins of a farm house in a town once known as Bearsville. His forces, and those of Marshal Stonewall Cogswell, were on the march but as yet their main bodies had not come in contact. Save for skirmishes between cavalry units, there had been no action. The ruined farm house had been a victim of an earlier fracas in this reservation which had seen in its comparatively brief time more combat than Belgium, that cockpit of Europe.

There was a sheen of oily moisture on the Baron's bulletlike head and his officers weren't particularly happy about it. Malcolm Haer characteristically went into a fracas with confidence, an aggressive confidence so strong that it often carried the day. In battles past, it had become a tradition that Haer's morale was worth a thousand men; the energy he expended was the despair of his doctors who had been warning him for a decade. But now, something was missing.

A forefinger traced over the military chart before them. "So far as we know, Marshal Cogswell has established his command here in Saugerties. Anybody have any suggestions as to why?"

A major grumbled, "It doesn't make much sense, sir. You know the marshal. It's probably a fake. If we have any superiority at all, it's our artillery."

"And the old fox wouldn't want to join the issue on the plains, down near the river," a colonel added. "It's his game to keep up into the mountains with his cavalry and light infantry. He's got Jack Alshuler's cavalry. Most experienced veterans in the field."

"I know who he's got," Haer growled in irritation. "Stop reminding me. Where in the devil is Balt?"

"Coming up, sir," Balt Haer said. He had entered only moments ago, a sheaf of signals in his hand. "Why didn't they make that date 1910, instead of 1900? With radio, we could speed up communications—"

His father interrupted testily. "Better still, why not make it 1945? Then we could speed up to the point where we could polish ourselves off. What have you got?"

Balt Haer said, his face in sulk, "Some of my lads based in West Hurley report concentrations of Cogswell's infantry and artillery near Ashokan reservoir."

"Nonsense," somebody snapped. "We'd have him."

The younger Haer slapped his swagger stick against his bare leg and kilt. "Possibly it's a feint," he admitted.

"How much were they able to observe?" his father demanded.

"Not much. They were driven off by a superior squadron. The Hovercraft forces are screening everything they do with heavy cavalry units. I told you we needed more—"

"I don't need your advice at this point," his father snapped. The older Haer went back to the map, scowling still. "I don't see what he expects to do, working out of Saugerties."

A voice behind them said, "Sir, may I have your permission—"

Half of the assembled officers turned to look at the newcomer.

Balt Haer snapped, "Captain Mauser. Why aren't you with your lads?"

"Turned them over to my second in command, sir," Joe Mauser said. He was standing to attention, looking at Baron Haer.

The Baron glowered at him. "What is the meaning of this cavalier intrusion, captain? Certainly, you must have your orders. Are you under the illusion that you are part of my staff?"

"No, sir," Joe Mauser clipped. "I came to report that I am ready to put into execution—"

"The great plan!" Balt Haer ejaculated. He laughed brittlely. "The second day of the fracas, and nobody really knows where old Cogswell is, or what he plans to do. And here comes the captain with his secret plan."

Joe looked at him. He said, evenly, "Yes, sir."

The Baron's face had gone dark, as much in anger at his son, as with the upstart cavalry captain. He began to growl ominously, "Captain Mauser, rejoin your command and obey your orders."

Joe Mauser's facial expression indicated that he had expected this. He kept his voice level however, even under the chuckling scorn of his immediate superior, Balt Haer.

He said, "Sir, I will be able to tell you where Marshal Cogswell is, and every troop at his command."

For a moment there was silence, all but a stunned silence. Then the major who had suggested the Saugerties field command headquarters were a fake, blurted a curt laugh.

"This is no time for levity, captain," Balt Haer clipped. "Get to your command."

A colonel said, "Just a moment, sir. I've fought with Joe Mauser before. He's a good man."

"Not that good," someone else huffed. "Does he claim to be clairvoyant?"

Joe Mauser said flatly. "Have a semaphore man posted here this afternoon. I'll be back at that time." He spun on his heel and left them.

Balt Haer rushed to the door after him, shouting, "Captain! That's an order! Return—"

But the other was obviously gone. Enraged, the younger Haer began to shrill commands to a noncom in the way of organizing a pursuit.

His father called wearily, "That's enough, Balt. Mauser has evidently taken leave of his senses. We made the initial mistake of encouraging this idea he had, or thought he had."

"*We?*" his son snapped in return. "I had nothing to do with it."

"All right, all right. Let's tighten up, here. Now, what other information have your scouts come up with?"

CHAPTER IX

At the Kingston airport, Joe Mauser rejoined Max Mainz, his face drawn now.

"Everything go all right?" the little man said anxiously.

"I don't know," Joe said. "I still couldn't tell them the story. Old Cogswell is as quick as a coyote. We pull this little caper today, and he'll be ready to meet it tomorrow."

He looked at the two-place sailplane which sat on the tarmac. "Everything all set?"

"Far as I know," Max said. He looked at the motorless aircraft. "You sure you been checked out on these things, captain?"

"Yes," Joe said. "I bought this particular soaring glider more than a year ago, and I've put almost a thousand hours in it. Now, where's the pilot of that light plane?"

A single-engined sports plane was attached to the glider by a fifty-foot nylon rope. Even as Joe spoke, a youngster poked his head from the plane's window and grinned back at them. "Ready?" he yelled.

"Come on, Max," Joe said. "Let's pull the canopy off this thing. We don't want it in the way while you're semaphoring."

A figure was approaching them from the Administration Building. A uniformed man, and somehow familiar.

"A moment, Captain Mauser!"

Joe placed him now. The Sov-world representative he'd met at Balt Haer's table in the Upper bar a couple of days ago. What was his name? Colonel Arpàd. Lajos Arpàd.

The Hungarian approached and looked at the sailplane in interest. "As a representative of my government, a military attache checking upon possible violations of the Universal Disarmament Pact, may I request what you are about to do, captain?"

Joe Mauser looked at him emptily. "How did you know I was here and what I was doing?"

The Sov colonel smiled gently. "It was by suggestion of Marshal Cogswell. He is a great man for detail. It disturbed him that an ... what did he call it? ... an *old pro* like yourself should join with Vacuum Tube Transport, rather than Continental Hovercraft. He didn't think it made sense and suggested that possibly you had in mind some scheme that would utilize weapons of a post 1900 period in your efforts to bring success to Baron Haer's forces. So I have investigated, Captain Mauser."

"And the marshal knows about this sail plane?" Joe Mauser's face was blank.

"I didn't say that. So far as I know, he doesn't."

"Then, Colonel Arpàd, with your permission, I'll be taking off."

The Hungarian said, "With what end in mind, captain?"

"Using this glider as a reconnaissance aircraft."

"Captain, I warn you! Aircraft were not in use in warfare until—"

But Joe Mauser cut him off, equally briskly. "Aircraft were first used in combat by Pancho Villa's forces a few years previous to World War I. They were also used in the Balkan Wars of about the same period. But those were powered craft. This is a glider, invented and in use before the year 1900 and hence open to utilization."

The Hungarian clipped, "But the Wright Brothers didn't fly even gliders until—"

Joe looked him full in the face. "But you of the Sov-world do not admit that the Wrights were the first to fly, do you?"

The Hungarian closed his mouth, abruptly.

Joe said evenly, "But even if Ivan Ivanovitch, or whatever you claim his name was, didn't invent flight of heavier than air craft, the glider was flown variously before 1900, including Otto Lilienthal in the 1890s, and was designed as far back as Leonardo da Vinci."

The Sov-world colonel stared at him for a long moment, then gave an inane giggle. He stepped back and flicked Joe Mauser a salute. "Very well, captain. As a matter of routine, I shall report this use of an aircraft for reconnaissance purposes, and undoubtedly a commission will meet to investigate the propriety of the departure. Meanwhile, good luck!"

Joe returned the salute and swung a leg over the cockpit's side. Max was already in the front seat, his semaphore flags, maps and binoculars on his lap. He had been staring in dismay at the Sov officer, now was relieved that Joe had evidently pulled it off.

Joe waved to the plane ahead. Two mechanics had come up to steady the wings for the initial ten or fifteen feet of the motorless craft's passage over the ground behind the towing craft.

Joe said to Max, "did you explain to the pilot that under no circumstances was he to pass over the line of the military reservation, that we'd cut before we reached that point?"

"Yes, sir," Max said nervously. He'd flown before, on the commercial lines, but he'd never been in a glider.

They began lurching across the field, slowly, then gathering speed. And as the sailplane took speed, it took grace. After it had been pulled a hundred feet or so, Joe eased back the stick and it slipped gently into the air, four or five feet off the ground. The towing airplane was still taxiing, but with its tow airborne it picked up speed quickly. Another two hundred feet and it, too, was in the air and beginning to climb. The glider behind held it to a speed of sixty miles or so.

At ten thousand feet, the plane leveled off and the pilot's head swiveled to look back at them. Joe Mauser waved to him and dropped the release lever which ejected the nylon rope from the glider's nose. The plane dove away, trailing the rope behind it. Joe knew that the plane pilot would later drop it over the airport where it could easily be retrieved.

In the direction of Mount Overlook he could see cumulus clouds and the dark turbulence which meant strong updraft. He headed in that direction.

Except for the whistling of wind, there is complete silence in a soaring glider. Max Mainz began to call back to his superior, was taken back by the volume, and dropped his voice. He said, "Look, captain. What keeps it up?"

Joe grinned. He liked the buoyance of glider flying, the nearest approach of man to the bird, and thus far everything was going well. He told Max, "An airplane plows through the air currents, a glider rides on top of them."

"Yeah, but suppose the current is going down?"

"Then we avoid it. This sailplane only has a gliding angle ratio of one to twenty-five, but it's a workhorse with a payload of some four hundred pounds. A really high performance glider can have a ratio of as much as one to forty."

Joe had found a strong updraft where a wind ran up the side of a mountain. He banked, went into a circling turn. The gauge indicated they were climbing at the rate of eight meters per second, nearly fifteen hundred feet a minute.

Max hadn't got the rundown on the theory of the glider. That was obvious in his expression.

Joe Mauser, even while searching the ground below keenly, went into it further. "A wind up against a mountain will give an updraft, storm clouds will, even a newly plowed field in a bright sun. So you go from one of these to the next."

"Yeah, great, but when you're between," Max protested.

"Then, when you have a one to twenty-five ratio, you go twenty-five feet forward for each one you drop. If you started a mile high, you could go twenty-five miles before you touched ground." He cut himself off quickly. "Look, what's that, down there? Get your glasses on it."

Max caught his excitement. His binoculars were tight to his eyes. "Sojers. Cavalry. They sure ain't ours. They must be Hovercraft lads. And look, field artillery."

Joe Mauser was piloting with his left hand, his right smoothing out a chart on his lap. He growled, "What are they doing there? That's at least a full brigade of cavalry. Here, let me have those glasses."

With his knees gripping the stick, he went into a slow circle, as he stared down at the column of men. "Jack Alshuler," he whistled in surprise. "The marshal's crack heavy cavalry. And several batteries of artillery." He swung the glasses in a wider scope and the whistle turned into a hiss of comprehension. "They're doing a complete circle of the reservation. They're going to hit the Baron from the direction of Phoenicia."

CHAPTER X

Marshal Stonewall Cogswell directed his old fashioned telescope in the direction his chief of staff indicated.

"What is it?" he grunted.

"It's an airplane, sir."

"Over a military reservation with a fracas in progress?"

"Yes, sir." The other put his glasses back on the circling object. "Then what is it, sir? Certainly not a free balloon."

"Balloons," the marshal snorted, as though to himself. "Legal to use. The Union forces had them toward the end of the Civil War. But practically useless in a fracas of movement."

They were standing before the former resort hotel which housed the marshal's headquarters. Other staff members were streaming from the building, and one of the ever-present Telly reporting crews were hurriedly setting up cameras.

The marshal turned and barked, "Does anybody know what in Zen that confounded thing, circling up there, is?"

Baron Zwerdling, the aging Category Transport magnate, head of Continental Hovercraft, hobbled onto the wooden veranda and stared with the others. "An airplane," he croaked. "Haer's gone too far this time. Too far, too far. This will strip him. Strip him, understand." Then he added, "Why doesn't it make any noise?"

Lieutenant Colonel Paul Warren stood next to his commanding officer. "It looks like a glider, sir."

Cogswell glowered at him. "A what?"

"A glider, sir. It's a sport not particularly popular these days."

"What keeps it up, confound it?"

Paul Warren looked at him. "The same thing that keeps a hawk up, an albatross, a gull —"

"A vulture, you mean," Cogswell snarled. He watched it for another long moment, his face working. He whirled on his chief of artillery. "Jed, can you bring that thing down?"

The other had been viewing the craft through field binoculars, his face as shocked as the rest of them. Now he faced his chief, and lowered the glasses, shaking his head. "Not with the artillery of pre-1900. No, sir."

"What can you do?" Cogswell barked.

The artillery man was shaking his head. "We could mount some Maxim guns on wagon wheels, or something. Keep him from coming low."

"He doesn't have to come low," Cogswell growled unhappily. He spun on Lieutenant Colonel Warren again. "When were they invented?" He jerked his thumb upward. "Those things."

Warren was twisting his face in memory. "Some time about the turn of the century."

"How long can the things stay up?"

Warren took in the surrounding mountainous countryside. "Indefinitely, sir. A single pilot, as long as he is physically able to operate. If there are two pilots up there to relieve each other, they could stay until food and water ran out."

"How much weight do they carry?"

"I'm not sure. One that size, certainly enough for two men and any equipment they'd need. Say, five hundred pounds."

Cogswell had his telescope glued to his eyes again, he muttered under his breath, "Five hundred pounds! They could even unload dynamite over our horses. Stampede them all over the reservation."

"What's going on?" Baron Zwerdling shrilled. "What's going on Marshal Cogswell?"

Cogswell ignored him. He watched the circling, circling craft for a full five minutes, breathing deeply. Then he lowered his glass and swept the assembled officers of his staff with an indignant glare. "Ten Eyck!" he grunted.

An infantry colonel came to attention. "Yes, sir."

Cogswell said heavily, deliberately. "Under a white flag. A dispatch to Baron Haer. My compliments and request for his terms. While you're at it, my compliments also to Captain Joseph Mauser."

Zwerdling was bug-eyeing him. "Terms!" he rasped.

The marshal turned to him. "Yes, sir. Face reality. We're in the dill. I suggest you sue for terms as short of complete capitulation as you can make them."

"You call yourself a soldier—!" the transport tycoon began to shrill.

"Yes, sir," Cogswell snapped. "A soldier, not a butcher of the lads under me." He called to the Telly reporter who was getting as much of this as he could. "Mr. Soligen, isn't it?"

The reporter scurried forward, flicking signals to his cameramen for proper coverage. "Yes, sir. Freddy Soligen, marshal. Could you tell the Telly fans what this is all about, Marshal Cogswell? Folks, you all know the famous marshal. Marshal Stonewall Cogswell, who hasn't lost a fracas in nearly ten years, now commanding the forces of Continental Hovercraft."

"I'm losing one now," Cogswell said grimly. "Vacuum Tube Transport has pulled a gimmick out of the hat and things have pickled for us. It will be debated before the Military Category Department, of course, and undoubtedly the Sov-world military attaches will have things to say. But as it appears now, the fracas as we have known it, has been revolutionized."

"Revolutionized?" Even the Telly reporter was flabbergasted. "You mean by that thing?" He pointed upward, and the lenses of the cameras followed his finger.

"Yes," Cogswell growled unhappily. "Do all of you need a blueprint? Do you think I can fight a fracas with that thing dangling above me, throughout the day hours? Do you understand the importance of reconnaissance in warfare?" His eyes glowered. "Do you think Napoleon would have lost Waterloo if he'd had the advantage of perfect reconnaissance such as that thing can deliver? Do you think Lee would have lost Gettysburg? Don't be ridiculous." He spun on Baron Zwerdling, who was stuttering his complete confusion.

"As it stands, Baron Haer knows every troop dispensation I make. All I know of his movements are from my cavalry scouts. I repeat, I am no butcher, sir. I will gladly cross swords with Baron Haer another day, when I, too, have ... what did you call the confounded things, Paul?"

"Gliders," Lieutenant Colonel Warren said.

CHAPTER XI

Major Joseph Mauser, now attired in his best off-duty Category Military uniform, spoke his credentials to the receptionist. "I have no definite appointment, but I am sure the Baron will see me," he said.

"Yes, sir." The receptionist did the things that receptionists do, then looked up at him again. "Right through that door, major."

Joe Mauser gave the door a quick double rap and then entered before waiting an answer.

Balt Haer, in mufti, was standing at a far window, a drink in his hand, rather than his customary swagger stick. Nadine Haer sat in an easy-chair. The girl Joe Mauser loved had been crying.

Joe Mauser, suppressing his frown, made with the usual amenities.

Balt Haer without answering them, finished his drink in a gulp and stared at the newcomer. The old stare, the aloof stare, an aristocrat looking at an underling as though wondering what made the fellow tick. He said, finally, "I see you have been raised to Rank Major."

"Yes, sir," Joe said.

"We are obviously occupied, major. What can either my sister or I possibly do for you?"

Joe kept his voice even. He said, "I wanted to see the Baron."

Nadine Haer looked up, a twinge of pain crossing her face.

"Indeed," Balt Haer said flatly. "You are talking to the Baron, Major Mauser."

Joe Mauser looked at him, then at his sister, who had taken to her handkerchief again. Consternation ebbed up and over him in a flood. He wanted to say something such as, "Oh *no*," but not even that could he utter.

Haer was bitter. "I assume I know why you are here, major. You have come for your pound of flesh, undoubtedly. Even in these hours of our grief—"

"I ... I didn't know. Please believe ..."

"... You are so constituted that your ambition has no decency. Well, Major Mauser, I can only say that your arrangement was with my father. Even if I thought it a reasonable one, I doubt if I would sponsor your ambitions myself."

Nadine Haer looked up wearily. "Oh, Balt, come off it," she said. "The fact is, the Haer fortunes contracted a debt to you, major. Unfortunately, it is a debt we cannot pay." She looked into his face. "First, my father's governmental connections do not apply to us. Second, six months ago, my father, worried about his health and attempting to avoid certain death taxes, transferred the family stocks into Balt's name. And Balt saw fit, immediately before the fracas, to sell all Vacuum Tube Transport stocks, and invest in Hovercraft."

"That's enough, Nadine," her brother snapped nastily.

"I see," Joe said. He came to attention. "Dr. Haer, my apologies for intruding upon you in your time of bereavement." He turned to the new Baron. "Baron Haer, my apologies for *your* bereavement."

Balt Haer glowered at him.

Joe Mauser turned and marched for the door which he opened then closed behind him.

On the street, before the New York offices of Vacuum Tube Transport, he turned and for a moment looked up at the splendor of the building.

Well, at least the common shares of the concern had skyrocketed following the victory. His rank had been upped to Major, and old Stonewall Cogswell had offered him a permanent position on his staff in command of aerial operations, no small matter of prestige. The difficulty was, he wasn't interested in the added money that would accrue to him, nor the higher rank—nor the prestige, for that matter.

He turned to go to his hotel.

An unbelievably beautiful girl came down the steps of the building. She said, "Joe."

He looked at her. "Yes?"

She put a hand on his sleeve. "Let's go somewhere and talk, Joe."

"About what?" He was infinitely weary now.

"About goals," she said. "As long as they exist, whether for individuals, or nations, or a whole species, life is still worth the living. Things are a bit bogged down right now, but at the risk of sounding very trite, there's tomorrow."